Notes to New Pastors

Notes to New Pastors

Ben R. Chamness

Abingdon Press
Nashville

NOTES TO NEW PASTORS

Copyright © 2008 by Abingdon Press

All rights reserved.

No part of this work may be reproduced or transmitted in any form or by any means, electronic or mechanical, including photocopying and recording, or by any information storage or retrieval system, except as may be expressly permitted by the 1976 Copyright Act or in writing from the publisher. Requests for permission should be addressed to Abingdon Press, P.O. Box 801, 201 Eighth Avenue South, Nashville, TN 37202-0801 or permissions@abingdonpress.com.

This book is printed on acid-free paper.

Library of Congress Cataloging-in-Publication Data

ISBN 978-1-426-70015-6

All scripture quotations unless noted otherwise are taken from the New Revised Standard Version of the Bible, copyright 1989, Division of Christian Education of the National Council of the Churches of Christ in the United States of America. Used by permission. All rights reserved.

Scripture quotations marked NASB are taken from the *New American Standard Bible.*® Copyright © 1960, 1962, 1963, 1968, 1971, 1972, 1973, 1975, 1977, 1995 by the Lockman Foundation. Used by permission. (www.Lockman.org)

Articles were originally published in *The Central Link*, an edition of *The United Methodist Reporter* for the Central Texas Conference of The United Methodist Church. Used by permission.

08 09 10 11 12 13 14 15 16 17--10 9 8 7 6 5 4 3 2 1

MANUFACTURED IN THE UNITED STATES OF AMERICA

To Joye

*Whose love and support
have made my ministry possible.*

CONTENTS

Foreword by Bishop John Wesley Hardt 9
Preface 11
Introduction 15
Chapter I. Developing Dynamic Worship 19
Chapter II. Preaching the Word 23
Chapter III. Visionary Leadership 27
Chapter IV. Keeping the Main Thing the Main Thing 31
Chapter V. Involving the Laity 35
Chapter VI. Hands-on Ministry 39
Chapter VII. Teaching the Bible 43
Chapter VIII. Youth Ministry 47
Chapter IX. Recruiting Young People for Ministry 51
Chapter X. Personal Devotions 55
Chapter XI. Developing Relationships 59
Chapter XII. Friendship Among Colleagues 63
Chapter XIII. Supporting My Pastor 67
Chapter XIV. Saving for Retirement 71
Chapter XV. Trusting God 75
Notes 79

FOREWORD

Political analysts continue to remind us that voters are looking for authenticity in candidates who are seeking public office. Having known Ben Chamness throughout the years of his ministry, it is my honor and privilege to assure those who read the pages of this book that both his life and the clear language of this book are authentic and genuine.

My first memory of Ben Chamness became firmly fixed when one of his first district superintendents began talking about a young man in his district whom I should get to know.

A decade or two later Ben became a member of a small group of neighbor pastors who found fellowship, study, and tennis in a growing relationship. That group included my brother-in-law, my former associate pastor, and another colleague whose friendship with me had begun in our freshmen year in college. On a few occasions this group invited me to share their fellowship. This stimulating association is given further emphasis in chapters entitled "Developing Relationships" and "Friendships Among Colleagues."

From the small rural churches to larger congregations in urban areas, the ministry of Ben Chamness met the challenge of steadily increasing opportunities in a rapidly changing world. Following his ministry with the historic Marvin

FOREWORD

United Methodist Church in Tyler, Texas, he became the superintendent of one of the Houston districts, and that experience provided him with a season of preparation that was extremely beneficial when he became a general superintendent. Through it all he has maintained a pastoral concern and understanding that no strategy or program means anything unless it can be put into practice with authentic integrity in some local congregation.

Each of the topics addressed in this book has a plain and direct message that speaks to a basic need in our Christian witness, but the one chapter that strikes a critical need in the church today and provides an honest answer to that need is entitled, "Recruiting Young People for Ministry." That chapter alone is worth whatever investment any reader makes in letting this authentic witness reach future generations of readers.

Your life will be blessed as countless persons have been blessed by the wise counsel and authentic witness of Bishop Ben Chamness.

John Wesley Hardt, Bishop in Residence, Emeritus,
Perkins School of Theology, SMU

PREFACE

In the last year of my active ministry I undertook a process of reflection on my years in the United Methodist ministry. Specifically I engaged in reflecting on how I might have done my ministry differently. Looking for areas where I was weak or have since learned better, I sought to enunciate those for the benefit of any who might read my words. In some instances I simply reaffirmed what I had known all along and found to work very well. My hope is that this has not simply been a self-indulgent effort on my part, but that others may gain from my reflections and my insights that have come with years of experience.

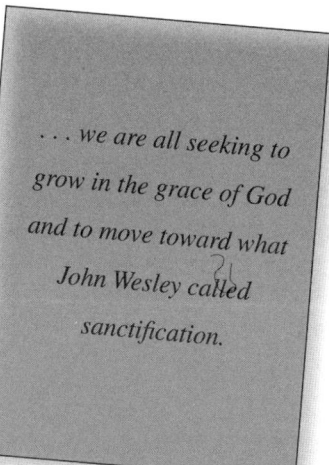

. . . we are all seeking to grow in the grace of God and to move toward what John Wesley called sanctification.

In these pages are compiled what first appeared as articles in the Central Texas Conference biweekly newspaper called the *Central Link*. As I began writing and these articles started appearing, I was encouraged to have them published for others to read. There were numerous persons who made a point to tell me that they found the self-reflection fascinating. Although I am gratified by those comments, it is my hope that young ministers as well as more seasoned pastors may

PREFACE

pick up on one or more of these ideas as areas on which they might seek to improve. Perhaps some lay persons will sense the struggle of their pastor and be more sympathetic, or perhaps they will find an area in which they can find growth and improvement. After all, we are all seeking to grow in the grace of God and to move toward what John Wesley called sanctification.

Ministry is so vital and can significantly impact human lives. Through all my years in ministry I have learned from others. If my life, my habits of ministry, or my shortcomings can help someone else to grow and strengthen their own life, that would be most gratifying.

I must say that I have been greatly blessed. The church has given me a place to live out my life. It has educated me and formed me. It has provided me and my family with a livelihood. It has given me larger areas of responsibility than I dared dream possible. It has cradled me, given me security, and provided me a place and a way to grow mentally and spiritually. So if I can contribute in some small way to its improvement and its future, that would be an additional blessing.

It has been my pleasure to serve the church in many capacities through the years. After I answered God's call to the ministry of what was then The Methodist Church (later to become The United Methodist Church) in 1959, I served four years as a student pastor. By that I mean that I attended

PREFACE

college or seminary while I also served as the pastor of a small membership church. Then in 1963, I was ordained as deacon and admitted to probationary membership in the Texas Conference of The Methodist Church. In 1965 I was ordained an elder and admitted into full membership in the same conference. From that time until 1996, it was my pleasure to serve as the pastor of several churches in Texas— Methodist or United Methodist churches in Avinger, Maud, Jacinto City, Missouri City, Port Arthur, Kingwood, and Tyler. From 1996-2000, I served at the pleasure of Bishop J. Woodrow Hearn as the District Superintendent of the Houston Northwest District. Then in the year 2000 the South Central Jurisdiction of The United Methodist Church saw fit to elect me to the office of bishop and assigned me to be the resident bishop of the Central Texas Conference where I served until retirement in 2008. It is from those years and those experiences that I draw in these vignettes on how I might go about my ministry if I could live my life over.

INTRODUCTION

> None of us is fortunate enough to live our lives a second time.... But if I could, I see some places where I would make some changes. There are other places where I have found my choices being confirmed as the appropriate or best choices at the time and under the given set of circumstances.

Almost thirteen months before I faced mandatory retirement, I received an e-mail from a woman in the conference with whom I had communicated a few times in the seven years I had been in Fort Worth. She started by saying, "I do not know if you are still there. I have heard that you are retired or retiring." It seems that in the last few months of my ministry people became more conscious of the fact that I faced mandatory retirement in August of 2008. With a year to go, it was my intention to still be very engaged for several more months—especially since we were preparing to host the General Conference in the Spring of 2008 and would have another Annual Conference session prior to my move to a different relationship. Jurisdictional Conference remained on the calendar as well.

In recent months more than one or two had mentioned to me my impending retirement . Bishop J. Woodrow Hearn, who was not ready for retirement when it came for him in the year 2000, asked me before it faced me, if I would not like to put that off. My response to him was like this: "Well, I have

INTRODUCTION

mixed emotions about it. I can see some positive things about retirement, but we have grown to love the people of the Fort Worth area."

By the time I reach that magic date when the church says that I must retire from active ministry, I will have served more than 45 years in the effective relationship with The United Methodist Church. Prior to that, I served four years as a student pastor. So this has become a way of life for me over the last half century. It has been a very fulfilling and exhilarating career. And I believe, by God's grace, that it has been a fruitful ministry.

Never have I doubted my call to the ministry. God spoke to me in such a clear and convincing manner. Certainly there have been times when I questioned why God called me to this ministry. There have been times of uncertainty and doubt about accomplishing some monumental task. But I could always reflect on God's call and God's ability to empower and see us through any project or any circumstance.

None of us is fortunate enough to live our lives a second time. None of us gets a second chance at life. None of us is able to redo aspects of our lives where we see that improvements could have been made, or errors in judgment could be corrected, or better choices would have made life richer or better. But if I could, I see some places where I would make some changes. There are other places where I have found my choices being confirmed as the appropriate or best

INTRODUCTION

choices at the time and under the given set of circumstances.

So as I entered the last year of my active ministry, I decided to write a series of articles for the *Central Link* that are a bit of reflection, a bit of confession, and a bit of challenge. The theme of these vignettes became: "If I Could Do My Ministry Over . . ." These articles have been collected here for a wider audience. I hope these reflections will be helpful, especially to young pastors and to laity who serve the church so faithfully and unselfishly.

Chapter I

DEVELOPING DYNAMIC WORSHIP

> *If I had my ministry to do over, I would start early developing dynamic worship experiences that would unite the various acts of worship, building upon the theme of that particular worship service.*

But the hour is coming, and is now here, when the true worshipers will worship the Father in spirit and truth, for the Father seeks such as these to worship him. God is spirit, and those who worship him must worship in spirit and truth. (Jn. 4: 23-24)

Worship is the central and defining experience in the life of a congregation. Therefore, it should be treated as such. All other church activities—fellowship dinners, educational pursuits, evangelistic tasks, missional emphases, and so forth—should emanate from and point back toward worship. From our experience with God, we are inspired to make disciples and to serve others. Out of gratitude for the love of God, we reach out. Then our experiences in serving God drive us back to celebrate those experiences as we bring our worship to God.

Too often in our celebration we respond as if the acts of

worship are unrelated. The hymns and the sermon should reflect a common theme that is developed around the scripture for the day. The liturgy should be an instrument to involve the worshipers in an act that reflects the spirit of the whole worship experience. Worship should involve the heart and the mind. As Jesus said, "God is spirit, and those who worship him must worship in spirit and truth" (Jn. 4:24).

Several years after I began my ministry I became aware of the value and the joy of developing a theme for each worship service. We do not simply sing some songs to warm up people for the sermon. No, the scripture for the day should provide the theme around which the music is selected, the liturgy is formed, and the sermon is developed. It is helpful for the preacher, the worship leader, the music director, and others to sit down and think together about the theme for the worship service. Then the elements of the service can be planned accordingly.

So if I had my ministry to do over, I would start early developing dynamic worship experiences that would unite the various acts of worship in bringing the desired effect of building upon the theme of that particular worship service. It is easy to see this approach taking place with regard to a Christmas Eve worship service, or with regard to an Easter morning worship service. But it is also effective on any given Sunday of the Christian year by using the scripture lesson(s) for that day and developing the theme accordingly. More dynamic worship occurs when some thought is put into the planning.

DEVELOPING DYNAMIC WORSHIP

People usually see and appreciate the unified thread in the worship experience.

I believe that the approach I have described will work in the traditional or the contemporary worship experience. A great deal of experimentation has been done with contemporary forms of worship in the last two or three decades. Some elements have proven helpful, and others need to be discarded. The measure of the effectiveness of a worship experience is the degree to which the service helps the worshipers celebrate the good news of Jesus Christ with the heart and the mind, or as Jesus said, "in spirit and truth."

Worship is vital for the individual and for the community of faith. Therefore, appropriate time must be given to make it meaningful and dynamic. When people experience that kind of worship, they want to come back for more.

Chapter II

PREACHING THE WORD

But how are they to call on one in whom they have not believed? And how are they to believe in one of whom they have never heard? And how are they to hear without someone to proclaim him? And how are they to proclaim him unless they are sent? As it is written, "How beautiful are the feet of those who bring good news!" (Rom. 10:14-15)

> So even though I focused on making preaching an important part of my ministry, if I could do my ministry over, I would make sure it came first and foremost in every setting.

With the perspective of nearly a half century of ministry, it has been obvious to me for a long time that quality preaching is vital for a pastor in any age and in any setting. People want someone to stand before them and deliver a clear and concise word of God that is applicable to their daily lives. They want a preacher to enunciate God's Word in a way that rings true and that makes a difference in their lives.

That ability is needed in every size church. It becomes more pronounced in larger churches. For some people the only

NOTES TO NEW PASTORS

time they encounter the pastor is on Sunday morning in the worship service, so it is vital that the preacher deliver the message as aptly as possible. In each generation there seems to be a different emphasis in preaching style. For instance, when I was starting, there was a demand for well-structured phrases and good grammar that caught people's attention. So the use of a manuscript or a rather full set of notes was in vogue. But in this day people seem more interested in words that communicate—action words, vision words, and word-pictures. They want concepts more than phrases. They want life stories and God's story. So these tend to communicate better without manuscripts and notes.

But whatever the method used, ample preparation is very important, and good communication skills amplify the message. In any case, it is certainly important to invest oneself in the message although the messenger must point beyond oneself. The message must be about God as revealed to us in Jesus Christ and as made known in the Holy Spirit.

If I could do my ministry over, I would start very early writing down illustrations and cataloguing them for future use in sermons. Whether they are recorded on card files or in the computer is immaterial. The point is that a good human interest story—preferably from personal experience—helps the hearers to identify with the message. Across the months and years one loses those stories, quotations, and other illustrative material if there is not some organized way to keep it and have it easily available when needed. As every pastor

PREACHING THE WORD

knows, it is important to read books, commentaries, magazines, newspapers; to see movies; to experience life with parishioners—in addition to being an avid student of the Scriptures—in order to bring all that one can to the sermon.

If I could start over, I would certainly protect more time each week for sermon preparation. Furthermore, I would continue to work on my delivery of the sermon. It is important to live with the Word of God until it comes alive, but it is just as important to make it understandable to those hearers in the pews.

Preachers have an awesome responsibility; namely, to deliver God's Word in a timely and fitting way to people in the church and community to which they have been assigned. They should have an urgency in their message, because God has empowered them to announce that "now is the acceptable time; see, now is the day of salvation!" (2 Cor. 6:2). So preaching should be aimed at decision-making by the hearer. The sermon should be delivered with an expectation that hearers will respond—even though they do not always show that outwardly.

I see some preachers today effectively using modern media to enhance their message. Others try to use it to their detriment. When handled well, it can connect the hearers and viewers with the contemporary world and bring God's Word to bear on it. But whether modern forms of media are used in the sermon or not, it is vital to connect the worshiper with

God. That is the central reason people come to worship. Preachers cannot compete with all the twenty-first-century video and audio experiences so readily available today. But we still have one thing that no one else has—that is the true and lively Word of God. When we are able to bring God's Word to bear in a relevant way on people's lives, we deliver something they cannot obtain anywhere else but in the church.

So even though I focused on making preaching an important part of my ministry, if I could do my ministry over, I would make sure it came first and foremost in every setting.

Chapter III

VISIONARY LEADERSHIP

Where there is no vision, the people are unrestrained. (Prov. 29:18, NASB)

> *If I had my ministry to do over, I would have started earlier utilizing the prophetic role as well as the priestly role. I would have exercised visionary leadership as well as preaching and meeting the pastoral needs of the congregation.*

When I first started my ministry, it seemed that preaching every Sunday and tending to the pastoral needs of the congregational members were the only requirements to have an effective ministry. Like those before me and those around me, I followed that path in my first few years of ministry. Then it seems that we went through a few years of ministry by management from the corner office as well. In this expectation the pastor oversaw staff members and volunteers in meeting the needs of ministry and mission.

It was a few years later that visionary leadership came into vogue. In the secular world and in the church, we began to recognize that strong leaders were able to cast a vision and get people to follow them. I think that much earlier I had elements of visioning in my ministry, but I had not cultivated them. In planning my ministry I could see what needed to be done and where the church needed to go, but I did little to share that vision or to incorporate people into it.

Increasingly it has become important that a pastor give visionary leadership. That kind of leadership has a place historically as well. It grows out of the prophetic role of ministry. The prophet was able to envision what was going to happen to God's people and to warn them. The pastoral role is more associated with the historical priestly function of ministry. So we have evolved into a combination of both the priestly and the prophetic roles being combined in an effective ministry in the twenty-first–century. This is a fuller and more comprehensive ministry.

If I had my ministry to do over, I would have started earlier utilizing the prophetic role as well as the priestly role. I would have exercised visionary leadership as well as preaching and meeting the pastoral needs of the congregation. The best visionary leadership begins with the question: What does God want us to do in this time and place? It involves the pastor first asking that question and finding an answer that can be shared with the other leaders of the congregation. Through discussion, prayer, and discernment, the people help to refine that vision of the pastor. Then it becomes the focus of the congregation. All energies and resources begin to follow the vision until it is accomplished.

In churches in which I exercised that visionary leadership,

VISIONARY LEADERSHIP

there was a unity of purpose and a greater sense of accomplishment. In the Central Texas Conference where I met with some of the leadership of the conference in the first few months and my goals and those of the conference were meshed, we began to develop a shared vision for the conference over the next two quadrennia. To a large measure we moved together to fulfill those goals. Visionary leadership should be a significant part of ministry.

Chapter IV

KEEPING THE MAIN THING THE MAIN THING

> *If I could do my ministry over, I believe that I would still be rigid in keeping my political preferences to myself while ministering in a nonpolitical way.*

Then the Pharisees went and plotted to entrap him in what he said. So they sent their disciples to him, along with the Herodians, saying, "Teacher, we know that you are sincere, and teach the way of God in accordance with truth, and show deference to no one; for you do not regard people with partiality. Tell us, then, what you think. Is it lawful to pay taxes to the emperor, or not?" But Jesus, aware of their malice, said, "Why are you putting me to the test, you hypocrites? Show me the coin used for the tax." And they brought him a denarius. Then he said to them, "Whose head is this, and whose title?" They answered, "The emperor's." Then he said to them, "Give therefore to the emperor the things that are the emperor's, and to God the things that are God's." (Matt. 22:15-21)

Early in my ministry I was serving a church in a community not far from Lone Star Steel Company. Prior to my arrival there had been a sharp disagreement at this plant that brought serious discord between the union employees and the management. One side was pitted against the other. There had been threats against lives. In fact, there had been shots fired into a home or two.

I discovered quickly that we had church members on each side of the ongoing argument. So I came to recognize that it was best not to take sides on this issue. It was my responsibility to be a pastor to all the people in my church and community. If I had taken either side of the issue, I would have immediately alienated all those on the other side of the issue. Then they would not have allowed me to be their pastor, and they would have been cut off from their church.

Through the years of my ministry I have refrained from endorsing candidates for public office—whether they are local, state, or national offices. Again if I took a public stand for a candidate, it is highly likely that there would be someone in my church who would oppose that candidate. If so, that person might either find it difficult to talk to me about spiritual matters because he or she would be blinded by my political stance. My perception and practice has been to refrain from personal alignments that might get in the way of my witness to someone about the gospel of Jesus Christ. My primary reason for being assigned as pastor of a church was to be the pastor of all the people.

That does not mean that I could never take stances on issues that adversely affected people. In fact, I spoke out against

KEEPING THE MAIN THING THE MAIN THING

gambling when the state was voting whether to make it legal because I knew there would be people with gambling addictions who would be most in peril. Often those are poor people who can least afford to lose their paycheck to gambling. There have been other issues that had a clear moral base to defend. But I have been careful to question my motivation before getting involved.

Certainly I have preferences in elections, and I cast my vote; but I try not to make my preferences public. Early in my married life, we moved one year in October just before the elections. Joye and I drove back to our previous voting district some one hundred miles round trip in order to vote in the senatorial race. Only after we came out of the voting booth did we discuss with each other for whom we voted. It turned out that we drove all that way and cancelled each other's vote. Since then, we have discussed our voting preferences with each other in advance. But it has been in the privacy of our home, not in the public arena.

If I could do my ministry over, I believe that I would still be rigid in keeping my political preferences to myself while ministering in a nonpolitical way. Even Jesus displayed that stance. You remember that the Scribes and Pharisees were the political parties of Jesus' time. They tried to get Him to take sides on religious traditions, taxes, and Roman authority. But Jesus would not do so. He told them to render to Caesar the things that are Caesar's, and render to God the things that are God's. Jesus had His eyes fixed on God's will, and He would not allow either party to get Him off track.

Pastors must be careful to keep the main thing the main thing. We must not allow a political candidate or personal issue to get in the way of our ministry to the Word of God.

Chapter V

INVOLVING THE LAITY

> *If I could do my ministry over, I would find additional ways to equip and involve laity in tasks of ministry.*

To the church of the Thessalonians.... We must always give thanks to God for you, brothers and sisters, as is right, because your faith is growing abundantly, and the love of everyone of you for one another is increasing. Therefore we ourselves boast of you among the churches of God for your steadfastness and faith.' (2 Thes. 1:1, 3-4a)

If I could do my whole ministry over, I would place greater emphasis from start to finish on the ministry of all Christians and give specific notice to the valuable role of the laity. As *The Book of Discipline of The United Methodist Church* says: "All Christians are called through their baptism to this ministry of servanthood in the world to the glory of God and for human fulfillment. The forms of this ministry are diverse in locale, in interest, and in denominational accent, yet always catholic in spirit and outreach."[1]

The church would not exist without the laity. Christ is the heartbeat of the church, and the laos (laity) are the breath of

NOTES TO NEW PASTORS

the church. From the laity come those who are set aside to be the clergy. They are set aside for specific tasks of ministry, the chief of which is to enable the laity to do their ministry in the name and spirit of Jesus Christ.

Too often clergy begin to think they are to do the ministry of the church, and too often the laity find it easier to allow the clergy to do their ministry than to personally engage in real service to people and the worship of God. The pastor is the shepherd of the local church, giving vision, leadership, encouragement, and support for the laity in their ministry. The pastor teaches and preaches the Word of God; the laity study and follow the Word of God.

It has been my experience that lay men and women are looking for places of meaningful service to God and humanity. As they get engaged in tasks of ministry, they begin to sense the joy of serving God. They usually take their tasks seriously. As they are informed and guided, they become great vessels of God at work among the people. This has been seen for a long time as some agree to teach a Sunday school class and continue to do so because their lives are enriched as they offer what they have to others who are learning and growing in faith. This has been seen by people who are uniquely gifted with beautiful voices, a sense of timing, and the ability to carry a tune. They join a choir and add their melodious voice to others in praising God and leading the congregation in worship.

INVOLVING THE LAITY

In the 1980s I developed a team of lay men and women who were trained and supervised in giving pastoral care in the Kingwood United Methodist Church. It was part of my doctoral project at Drew University. As a result of the project, I was able to write a doctoral thesis on *Developing a Program of Training and Supervision for a Team of Laity Involved in Pastoral Care*. Also as a result of the project, the laity involved as part of the team met with me biweekly to give oral reports of their contacts. One of them was asked at each meeting to share a case study so that the whole group could reflect on it. This group made hospital calls, shut-in visits, follow-up calls to grieving families, and so forth. They agreed early that their ministry had elements of confidentiality and they would be expected to honor those.

By training the congregation at the same time in what they could expect from this team of pastoral care givers among the laity, we found that they were able to provide meaningful and helpful care to their fellow members. They also found that many of the principles they used in this ministry they could also use with their associates at work or in the community. All of us recognized that the needs for pastoral ministry were far too many for the pastor to take care of all of them. The pastor usually was involved in crisis situations, but the pastor could not be at all places at all times. The addition of several laity in this ministry greatly expanded our ministry.

This is only one area in which laity can be better equipped to serve God. If I could do my ministry over, I would find additional ways to equip and involve laity in tasks of ministry. The lay people are a valuable resource. Many of them are willing, but they need to have the doors opened, the way described, and the encouragement to be engaged.

Chapter VI

HANDS-ON MINISTRY

> *If I could do my ministry over, I would involve laity in meaningful tasks of ministry and reduce the time spent in committee meetings. I believe people today want to do something that makes a difference.*

But be doers of the word, and not merely hearers who deceive themselves. For if any are hearers of the word and not doers, they are like those who look at themselves in a mirror; for they look at themselves and, on going away, immediately forget what they were like. But those who look into the perfect law, the law of liberty, and persevere, being not hearers who forget but doers who act— they will be blessed in their doing.

If any think they are religious, and do not bridle their tongues but deceive their hearts, their religion is worthless. Religion that is pure and undefiled before God, the Father, is this: to care for orphans and widows in their distress, and to keep oneself unstained by the world. (James 1:22-27)

For many years I was an ardent advocate of committees and councils and boards for everything in the local church. I set up committees where they were not already organized. The Board of Trustees was not enough; we organized a Parsonage Committee and a Kitchen Committee, as well as a Building Use Committee. They all had functions to oversee and met periodically to consider and discuss a plan, a schedule, and the level of activity in which they would need to be engaged. The Worship Committee had subcommittees for the Altar Guild, the Usher Committee, and the Acolyte Committee. They all reported to the Worship Committee.

But in the mid 1990s I had a member of our church who was vice-president of one of the largest oil companies in Houston tell me that he was ready to be involved in some way. He asked me to find him a place to serve. So I began to ask him on which committee or board he would like to serve. His reply shocked me. He said, "No, I don't want to be on one of those. Through the years I have served on all the committees and boards. I want a place where I can do hands-on ministry. Just give me a place in the soup kitchen serving needy people."

After thinking about that conversation for a few days, I got together some of our key lay leaders and shared that experience with them. Then with their help we set about reorganizing the church. We reduced the number of people on the Board from more than one hundred members to twelve; we reduced the number and size of the committees. Then we developed ministry opportunities—places of service where people could do hands-on ministry. It was easy to develop a long list of tasks in which people could be engaged, perform a vital ministry, and often see results from their contribution

HANDS-ON MINISTRY

of time and effort. Those tasks included a wide variety of services, ranging from reading Scripture in the worship service to ushering, serving as acolytes, visiting members in the hospitals, rocking babies in the nursery, calling on shut-ins, doing carpentry, serving in soup kitchen lines, teaching Sunday school or Bible classes, and so forth.

We reoriented that local church to think of service in terms of hands-on ministry tasks instead of serving on a committee that met several times a year and often saw little or no result. The people in that church endorsed that concept and found greater satisfaction in their service.

If I could do my ministry over, I would take that approach, involving laity in meaningful tasks of ministry and reducing the time spent in committee meetings. I believe people today want to do something that makes a difference. They want to be engaged where their talents are useful. We need to help our people see their talents and to use those in ways that build up the church and the kingdom of God.

Chapter VII

TEACHING THE BIBLE

Teach them the statutes and instructions and make known to them the way they are to go and the things they are to do.
(Exod. 18:20)

> *If I had my ministry to do over, I would commit myself to teaching a class on some portion of the Bible each year.*

In the life of the Christian, Bible study needs to be a focal point. Whether we are simply trying to live our lives from day to day, whether we are seeking meaning in the midst of chaos, whether we are searching for the truths of God to impact the journey of our lives, whether we are trying to find solace in the midst of grief, or whether we are seeking material for a sermon, every Christian will find the Scriptures speak to them. We grow in knowledge and in grace as we pore over the pages of the Bible.

Yet some people open the Bible and having no understanding of the way it is laid out and the context in which the words were written and the way they should be understood, find they are overwhelmed or confused. Some lay down the book thinking the cause is futile. Therefore, structured Bible study is helpful to them. Once they gain insights, they are more able to read and better understand the words, especially if they have resources with which to work. Group study and discussion, however, is always helpful.

The letters of Paul were sent to churches and groups of churches. They were to be read in community with others. Ever since the Bible was canonized, people have studied the Scriptures together, usually being led by a person who was able to enlighten, inform, and inspire. Sometimes that was a priest or minister. Sometimes it has been a lay person. Even if the leader does not have all the answers, members of the group usually contribute to one another's understanding by sharing their understanding or experience that relates to the passage under consideration.

There were times in my ministry in which I led a Bible study for a few weeks at the time. Of course, the Bible was always central to my sermons. Weekly Bible study undergirded my preaching. However, as I now reflect back on my years in ministry, I believe I could have been more effective, and perhaps have enriched more lives, if I had consistently led a Bible study in my churches. I also believe that my life would have been enriched by those who participated in the Bible studies.

A few years ago a woman contacted me and told me that she was a member of one of my former churches and participated in a 34-week Bible study that I led several years prior

TEACHING THE BIBLE

to that time. She told me how that Bible study had helped her identify a call to ministry. At the time she wrote me, she said that she was in seminary and looking forward to pastoral ministry. She thanked me for leading that Bible study. She is now serving as a very effective pastor of a church.

Not everyone who attends a Bible study will find God calling them to ministry, but everyone will be enriched and nurtured and strengthened. Friendships will develop, and spiritual development will occur. Many will grow closer to God.

If I had my ministry to do over, I would commit myself to teaching a class on some portion of the Bible each year. Some pastors do this to develop leaders of their churches. Some do it to rightfully share the knowledge and insights they have gained in seminary, the church, and life experiences. Some intentionally determine to lead small groups of Bible study to enhance discussion, and they limit enrollment. Others open their Bible studies to anyone who will come. But pastors are, generally speaking, better trained and more equipped to lead Bible studies than most of the people in their congregations. That does not mean that laity should be supplanted in this task. Many of them have much to give and have influenced numerous lives across the years.

But too many pastors have neglected sharing their gifts as teachers. I believe that the pastor's involvement in this way speaks volumes about how important Bible study is for us all. It affords a wonderful way to get to know people and share significantly in their lives. It is a growing experience for leaders and students. But most importantly, the shared word of God becomes dynamic in our growth as Christians.

Chapter VIII

YOUTH MINISTRY

Let no one despise your youth, but set the believers an example in speech and conduct, in love, in faith, in purity. (1 Tim. 4:12)

> *I do not propose to have all the answers to youth ministry, but I do know that if I had my ministry to do over, I would spend more quality time with the youth in the church.*

If there is one area of the mainline churches' ministry that has been consistently weak over the past fifty years, it would have to be youth ministry. Unfortunately in many of our churches an intentional ministry to young people has been nearly non-existent. In other churches the frustrations have been frequent because the church has not been able to attract or keep youth involved in the life of the congregation.

On the other hand, in churches where the youth ministry has been vibrant and strong, the whole church has been significantly buoyed and energized. The church is usually more open to innovation, more willing to financially support their youth, and more engaged in things that matter to the younger generation. A respected staff member and energetic adult lay members who love young people are almost always engaged in the youth program that is successful.

NOTES TO NEW PASTORS

We have all seen the pattern of children starting out in church school and vacation Bible school; but by the time they get to high school, they have lost interest and dropped out of church participation. Or they come just to activities that the parents force them to attend. Then they go off to college, and/or they start a family. Before anyone knows it, they have been out of church for several years before they have children of their own and suddenly realize the children should have the benefit of religious education.

Someone has pointed out that the most dramatic shift in our culture over the last two or three generations has been the increased age at which men and women get married. That has had tremendous impact on a number of areas of our common life. Perhaps the impact is felt as much in the church as anywhere else. It means that people have children later in life, and that has traditionally brought young people back to church. So it is now longer between the time when young people drop out of church and the time they decide to come back to church. If and when they do return to the church, the average age of church attendees has increased.

But even more important, the teen years are very formative years, and the presence of the church in their lives can make a very significant impact on the decisions they make, the course of life they choose, and the satisfaction and fulfillment they attain in life. I am convinced that the high suicide rate could be reduced and the trafficking in drugs could be greatly reduced if the youth of our society had a sense that some adult(s) cared for them and if they were given encouragement and provided healthy environments for interaction with adults and youth with a message of hope and meaning.

One of the areas in which I tried to spend quality time with youth was in the annual confirmation classes. Whether the classes were large or small (and I taught groups numbering between 3 and 65), I found the youth eager to learn—especially if I made an effort to communicate on their level. When we were at Kingwood United Methodist Church, we had over 200 youth and their sponsors that participated in United Methodist Action Reachout by Methodist Youth (U.M. A.R.M.Y.). Cultivation of the program went on all year with the primary focus on a week of intense work, fun, and witness by the youth on construction sites working with residents of poor neighborhoods. The youth earned their money to make the trip, carried their own supplies, and spent a week in the hot sun repairing house roofs, floors, porches, and walls. They painted and cleaned yards. They engaged in conversation with the residents, and they usually had an opportunity to tell why their faith led them to make the sacrifice to be present. Often the residents expressed their sincere appreciation and talked about their faith. The youth came back from the experience very enthusiastic about their faith and their spiritual lives. (A very similar program for youth is conducted in the Central Texas Conference.)

I do not propose to have all the answers to youth ministry, but I do know that if I had my ministry to do over, I would spend more quality time with the youth in the families who attend church. I would try to learn more of their interests and show them that I could relate to their concerns. But I would also try to lead them to healthy and fulfilling choices that could open windows of hope and future development for them. I would find a way to show them how Jesus Christ is real in my life and how the Lord wants to be real in their lives.

Chapter IX

RECRUITING YOUNG PEOPLE FOR MINISTRY

> *If I had my ministry to do over, I would give some people who display gifts and graces for ministry a little more attention.*

Now the boy Samuel was ministering to the Lord under Eli... Then the LORD called, "Samuel! Samuel!" and he said, "Here I am!" and ran to Eli, and said, "Here I am, for you called me." But he said, "I did not call; lie down again." So he went and lay down. The LORD called again, "Samuel!" Samuel got up and went to Eli, and said, "Here I am, for you called me." But he said, "I did not call, my son; lie down again." Now Samuel did not yet know the LORD, and the word of the LORD had not yet been revealed to him. The LORD called Samuel again, a third time. And he got up and went to Eli, and said, "Here I am, for you called me." Then Eli perceived that the LORD was calling the boy. Therefore, Eli said to Samuel, "Go, lie down, and if he calls you, you shall say, 'Speak, LORD, for your servant is listening.' " So Samuel went and lay down in his place.

Now the LORD came and stood there, calling as before, "Samuel! Samuel!" And Samuel said, "Speak, for your servant is listening." Then the LORD said to Samuel, "See, I am

NOTES TO NEW PASTORS

about to do something in Israel that will make both ears of anyone who hears of it tingle." (1 Sam. 3:1, 4-11)

During my later teen years, my pastor's name was Rev. Conrad (Connie) Winborn. He was appointed to Rehobeth Methodist Church near Carthage, Texas; and he and his wife, Laura, moved there soon after he graduated from seminary. I finished high school and started my first year of college in my home town. During that freshman year I felt God's call to the ministry and decided to begin the journey into the ministry of the (then) Methodist Church. I wanted to serve God and follow God's will for my life. God was calling me to help people, and this was the door God opened for me.

I had been active in ministry forty-one years when the South Central Jurisdiction of The United Methodist Church saw fit to elect me to the office of Bishop. Before I moved to Fort Worth to which I had been assigned, I went to see my friend and mentor, who had now retired from the active ministry. I observed through the years that Rev. Winborn had received several young candidates for ministry. There had been three from Rehobeth Methodist Church during his time as pastor of that church, and there were a number of others in a variety of churches he later served.

I observed, "Connie, you have helped a lot of young people enter the ministry during your active years. Not all pastors have that kind of record. Can you tell me how you did it?"

RECRUITING YOUNG PEOPLE FOR MINISTRY

He seemed to be ready with the answer. He replied, "Ben, when I moved to a new church, I selected some young people whom I thought had gifts and graces for the ministry. I tried to spend time with them. I found ways to involve them in the life of the church. God did the rest."

> It is true that God calls us to ministry, but at times God can use some help to prepare the environment.

I began to rethink how he had, indeed, taken an interest in me when he came to Rehobeth, but it seemed at the time that he did that with other youth and adults. However, I did remember a few times when he invited me to read the scripture for the worship service, and a couple of times he invited me to go with him to visit church members in the hospitals. He also took me with him to visit shut-ins once. I never remember Connie asking me to consider the ministry. But I do remember that when I felt God tugging on me to make that decision, Connie was the first one I wanted to talk to about it. He told me then that he knew I was struggling with the decision. And he patiently led me to the next steps.

During the course of my ministry I have had a few people respond to God's call, but not nearly so many as Connie had. So if I had my ministry to do over, I would give some people who display gifts and graces for ministry a little more attention. It is true that God calls us to ministry, but at times God can use some help to prepare the environment.

NOTES TO NEW PASTORS

At a time when The United Methodist Church and most mainline denominations are in great need for more young clergy, I hope that this generation will do a better job than my generation in helping to identify talented and gifted young men and women to prepare for God to call to the ordained ministry. I can tell you that it is rewarding to see a person respond to the call to ministry as a result of something you have done or said. And certainly if the church is to continue to make a vital impact in future generations, there must be sufficient young men and women responding to God's claim on their lives.

One of the reasons the church is having difficulty reaching the younger generations is that our clergy are growing older. Younger people tend to identify more with younger clergy. So I recognize that I should have talked with Rev. Winborn about how he did it many years earlier. Perhaps it would have made a different impact on me, and thereby on several others who might have given more thought to a career in the ministry of the church, serving God and humanity.

Chapter X

PERSONAL DEVOTIONS

> *If I could do my ministry over, I would be more consistent in having a time of personal daily devotions.*

And whenever you pray, do not be like the hypocrites; for they love to stand and pray in the synagogues and at the street corners, so that they may be seen by others. Truly I tell you, they have received their reward. But whenever you pray, go into your room and shut the door and pray to your Father who is in secret; and your Father who sees in secret will reward you. (Matt. 6:5-6)

In the rush of life it is easy to put aside some important activities such as physical exercise and personal devotions. Each of these consumes time, but each should be a planned part of our daily lives. Just as thirty minutes of exercise every day can benefit the heart and the lungs, and help prevent heart disease, cancer, obesity, and other illnesses that plague humanity today, likewise a daily period of thirty minutes of spiritual devotional time can benefit the heart and the mind. A regular time apart with the Bible and resource materials can greatly improve the relationship with God and has proved beneficial in meeting the demands of life. No wonder

John Wesley included daily devotions as one of the spiritual disciplines of the Christian life.

Whether we are lay or clergy, a consistent time to study God's Word is a spiritual exercise from which we may gain sustenance for life. It is tempting for clergy to rationalize that their weekly sermon preparation is sufficient time to spend with study and deliberation of the Word of God. But as important as that time and effort is, it is not the same as time spent for personal devotions. As Rudy Rasmus says in his book *Touch: The Power of Touch in Transorming Lives*, "But my spiritual and emotional tank runs dry if I don't keep drinking of the Spirit's love and power. I trust His Spirit to fill me again and again with compassion, direction, and strength. I need it …I desperately need it because my old selfish nature is still alive and kicking (see Ephesians 4:20-24). I have a hundred choices a day to go in one direction or another—toward selfishness or toward love. I need the Holy Spirit's authority and compassion to fill me, direct me, and work through me."[1]

From time to time I have used different materials for my devotional time. At times I just read a chapter of the Bible and have personal prayer. Doing that, I have read through the Bible several times. But I also have been selective at times of the books of the Bible from which to read. For a period of time I had a daily prayer time and wrote in a journal of what my prayers consisted. Months later I reread my journal and was truly surprised at how many of the prayers I had uttered

PERSONAL DEVOTIONS

in intercession had come true. God does, indeed, answer prayer.

Prepared devotional materials can be good resources. At times I have used *The Upper Room* or other devotional guides. *A Guide to Prayer for All Who Seek God* by Norman Shawchuck and Reuben Job[2] is a helpful resource and guide to prayer based on the liturgical calendar. I have used this resource at times in conjunction with a covenant group in the Council of Bishops and with the cabinet of the Central Texas Conference. There is a wealth of materials to give guidance or to assist with daily devotions.

But most important is the commitment to set aside the time and to focus our attention on God, studying God's Word, offering up our prayers, and listening for God's voice. When we are willing to "Be still, and know that I am God" (Psalm 46:10a), it makes a tremendous difference in how we spend the remainder of our day. So if I could do my ministry over, I would be more consistent in having a time of personal daily devotions.

Chapter XI

DEVELOPING RELATIONSHIPS

> *If I could do my ministry over, I would spend every minute I could before a worship service visiting with the people.*

After this Paul left Athens and went to Corinth. There he found a Jew named Aquila, a native of Pontus, who had recently come from Italy with his wife Priscilla, because Claudius had ordered all Jews to leave Rome. Paul went to see them, and, because he was of the same trade, he stayed with them, and they worked together—by trade they were tentmakers. Every sabbath he would argue in the synagogue and would try to convince Jews and Greeks. . . .

Then he left the synagogue and went to the house of a man named Titius Justus, a worshiper of God; his house was next door to the synagogue. Crispus, the official of the synagogue, became a believer in the Lord, together with all his household; and many of the Corinthians who heard Paul became believers and were baptized. (Acts: 18:1-4, 7-8)

Building relationships is a vital part of ministry—even in an itinerant system. Ministry is done in relationship with other people. It is seldom, if ever, done in isolation.

NOTES TO NEW PASTORS

Early in my ministry I spent a great deal of time getting to know people. I visited in people's homes. Sometimes I visited them at work. In fact, I had a goal of being in every church member's home in the first year (or sooner when I had small churches). But as I moved to larger churches, that became more difficult. As culture changed and the husband and wife were often both in the workforce, it became less expected (and often less desirable) for the pastor to visit in the home. So it became easier to tell myself that I could spend my time more wisely by studying for my sermon, directing the church staff, or preparing an agenda for a board or committee meeting.

One of the things I have observed, as I have been able in more recent years to visit different churches, is how some pastors are very good at visiting with church members and visitors as they gather for worship. Some of them spend time in the sanctuary saying hello to different people until the very time for the worship service to start. I like to visit with people, but I developed a habit of spending the last five or ten minutes meditating on my sermon for one last time, or getting the clergy and choir together for prayer before we entered the sanctuary. But if I could do my ministry over, I would spend every minute I could before a worship service visiting with the people. Especially in larger churches, the pastor does not have an opportunity to see some of them at any other time.

It is amazing how people will follow a leader with whom they have a good strong relationship. Even national leaders,

DEVELOPING RELATIONSHIPS

if they are successful, build a relationship of trust with their constituents via the media. They speak the truth in all sincerity, and they obviously work for the common good. And the longer we can see them doing that, the more we tend to trust them.

The laity in our churches want a pastor with whom they can relate and to whom they can go in trust and confidence. They want a pastor who will hear their concerns, and who will reveal the truth of the gospel as they lead them in their Christian pursuit. They want the leader of their church to be someone who knows them. Being with them at the time of a family baptism, wedding, or funeral is one good way to build relationships. Visiting them in the hospital or at home if there is an extended illness goes a long way. It says: "I care, . . . the church cares, . . . God cares."

Even in my first eighteen months as a bishop, I committed myself to visiting all the churches in the Central Texas Conference because I wanted to meet as many of the people as possible and actually see the church locations. Also, since that time I have spent as many weekends as I could in the churches meeting people and building relationships. Nothing replaces good relationships when it comes to ministry.

Chapter XII

FRIENDSHIPS AMONG COLLEAGUES

> *If I had my ministry to do over, I would certainly be conscientious about developing friends among the United Methodist clergy in the area where I was serving.*

Paul, an apostle of Christ Jesus by the will of God, and Timothy our brother, to the saints and faithful brothers and sister in Christ in Colossae; grace to you and peace from God our Father. . . . Tychicus will tell you all the news about me; he is a beloved brother, a faithful minister, and a fellow servant in the Lord. . . . Luke, the beloved physician, and Demas greet you. (Col. 1:1-2; 4:7, 14)

During most of my college years and all of my seminary years, I had fellow students who were colleagues in ministry as well. We served as pastors of local churches on the weekend while attending classes during the week. We had a good bit in common, and we would often share our experiences with each other. Our friendship expanded, and some of those fellow students and colleagues remained friends all our lives.

NOTES TO NEW PASTORS

After I started serving a church full time, I found it helpful to get to know pastors of other United Methodist churches in adjacent communities and in the district in which I was serving. In a couple of locations we developed a fellowship group or a study group, which met weekly. The fellowship group was open to any area United Methodist pastors who were available on a given morning to meet for coffee and open discussion. The study group used the lectionary to discuss and share insights and resources that might be helpful in developing the next Sunday sermon. It also gave us interaction with one another that we would never otherwise have had.

In a couple of places where I served, I devcloped a relationship with one or two other United Methodist pastors in which we would meet frequently for coffee and fellowship. We would share what was going on with us—our families, our churches, and so forth. The time provided a sounding board sometimes for ministries we were considering, celebrations for accomplishments in our churches, or support for one another when everything was not going well.

In one location there were four of us who linked up to play tennis early every Thursday morning. (We would usually finish and get back to our offices by 9:00 or 9:30 a.m.) We enjoyed each other's company as well as the exercise. After a couple of years we decided to get our wives together for dinner. That was enjoyable, so we planned to add that feature to our friendship once a month. For awhile everything was going wonderfully. Then the Bishop decided to appoint us to churches in different directions, thereby splitting us up geographically.

But we decided to get together once a quarter, have dinner, spend the night, and play tennis, over a night and a half day. And we followed that pattern until health became a problem for one and then another. But on the first quarterly gathering we went to Lake Elkins near Huntsville, Texas, where the four couples were able to stay in the guest house for free. The only obligation was that we must look at property before we left. The rain prevented our tennis game, but we went with a sales person who showed us property lots in the rain. All four couples bought lots that morning. Two lots were adjacent, and the other two were also adjacent but they were down the street a short distance. Eventually all four couples built retirement homes in Lake Elkins. Although two of the men and one of the women have now died, the others remain very good friends.

If I had my ministry to do over, I would certainly be conscientious about developing friends among the United Methodist clergy in the area where I was serving. There is a camaraderie that is unlike any other. Clergy often feel very lonely, even though they are dealing with and ministering to lay people all the time. Every pastor needs someone who understands him or her and the issues that are being faced, someone who has similar interests and who can be sensitive to their shared concerns.

Unfortunately I have seen some of my colleagues in ministry become ingrown or withdrawn. They are afraid to share with anyone, and they suffer needlessly. It is amazing what an hour or two each week with a colleague can do to lighten the load, to confirm some thoughts we were having, to challenge us to think about matters differently, and to share in a way that we know they have our welfare and the church's welfare at heart. And if there are no issues or concerns, it is just great to have another friend. We cannot have too many of them.

Chapter XIII

SUPPORTING MY PASTOR

John said to him, "Teacher, we saw someone casting out demons in your name, and we tried to stop him, because he was not following us." But Jesus said, "Do not stop him; for no one who does a deed of power in my name will be able soon afterward to speak evil of me. Whoever is not against us is for us. For truly I tell you, whoever gives you a cup of water to drink because you bear the name of Christ will by no means lose the reward." (Mk. 9:38-41)

> This is one area in which I am looking forward rather than backward, hoping not to have to say how I would do my ministry differently in hindsight.

As I moved toward retirement after more than forty-nine years in the United Methodist ministry—thirty-seven of them in the local parish, four as a District Superintendent, and eight as a bishop—I made a commitment to be supportive of my local pastor and of the bishop in the area where I am living. One of the most unfortunate things I have experienced a few times is seeing a retired pastor undermining the ministry of the local church pastor. Sometimes the retired pastor does not realize how much impact his or her negative words about the current pastor have.

NOTES TO NEW PASTORS

It occurs at times when the retired pastor agrees with a church member's criticism of the current pastor. It can occur when he or she comments about how different things were in his or her days as pastor of that church. It may occur even without criticism when a former pastor or retired pastor agrees to conduct a wedding or a funeral for a member of the church without the pastor asking them to do so. Even more unfortunate are the times when a retired pastor purposefully criticizes the current pastor.

Whatever the circumstances, it is inappropriate (and a chargeable offense) for any clergy to undermine the ministry of another clergy. That is a losing proposition for everyone involved—the offending clergy, the recipient of the criticism, and the church that is torn in the divisiveness.

Fortunately there are many former pastors who are very supportive of the current pastor of their former church, and there are numerous retired clergy that are helpful to the pastor of the church attended by the retiree. Others are far away and stay out of contact. Bishop Mike Coyner of Indiana tells of preaching one Sunday at Battle Ground United Methodist Church. The former pastor was participating in the service that day. The current pastor told the bishop about the former pastor: "He is so supportive and helpful to my ministry. He doesn't agree with everything I am doing here at his former church, but when he does have questions or concerns, he comes to me directly rather than complaining to any of our members. I deeply appreciate his support and his counsel for my ministry."

SUPPORTING MY PASTOR

As I prepared for a different relationship with the church—one in which I attend worship rather than lead it, one in which I am a participant in a community of faith rather than the leader of that community—I am making a commitment to:

1. Retire in a community in which I have never served as pastor, district superintendent, or bishop. We purposely made that decision because we know the temptations for the congregation's members to turn to me will not be as likely, and because I will not be able to compare the church to the way I remember it when I led it. The chances of remaining above any differences or disagreements will be less pronounced.

2. Be supportive of the pastor, whoever he or she may be. There is a special relationship between the pastor and the people, and I respect that and do not want to interrupt it in any way.

3. Speak to the pastor privately if I have a valid concern, but share that with no one else. My attempt will be to offer assistance and wisdom, not to interfere in any way.

4. Conduct no weddings or funerals in that local church or elsewhere without a direct invitation from the pastor or bishop.

5. Pray for the current pastor and the congregation. That is the very least I can do.

This is one area in which I am looking forward rather than backward, hoping not to have to say how I would do my ministry differently in hindsight.

Chapter XIV

SAVING FOR RETIREMENT

If you gathered nothing in your youth, / how can you find anything in your old age? (Sirach, 25:3 in the Apocrypha)

> *If I had my ministry to do over, I would handle my income differently. Joye and I covenanted early in our marriage to tithe ten percent of our income, and God has blessed us for that. But I would add to that formula to save ten percent from the beginning.*

It seemed like such a long time until retirement. After all, I was just starting my ministry. I was only nineteen years of age. I was only making $183.33 per month and I was paying for an automobile and my tuition and books at college. Why should I save money for retirement then?

Then I got married. I had heard that two can live as cheaply as one, but it did not work out that way. My wife needed shoes, dresses, shoes, purses, shoes, pantsuits, shoes, makeup, shoes, and food. And I wanted to give her everything she needed, and some of what she wanted. Retirement savings could wait.

Then we had a child, and before long we had two children. They needed cribs, baby seats, blankets, formula, diapers, and all kind of things. And as they grew, each year they

71

needed something new and different. Then they started to school. We had to buy school supplies and clothes. We did not have enough money to put away for retirement. That must wait.

Before long our two sons were out of school, and we were getting older. It was time that we started to think seriously about setting aside some money for our retirement. But by starting so late, how could we ever put aside enough to support us in our later years? It seemed impossible.

After all, we had lived all our adult lives on a frugal minister's salary. Sure, Joye had worked a few years while our sons were in school, but most of that income was set aside to buy necessities for our boys. So we were starting late in setting aside any savings that would provide for the two of us in our sunset years.

As significant as each demand upon our money was in those first several years, if I had my ministry to do over, I would begin early—yes at the very beginning—to save for retirement. When a person gets closer to retirement, one sees how important it is to start early and contribute regularly to a fund that prepares for those later years. After the productive years, there is no way to produce income for the necessities, much less for any luxuries of life. If we did not adequately prepare along the way, our lifestyle might have to change for the worse.

SAVING FOR RETIREMENT

Financial managers and retirement consultants can show us how it is to our great advantage to save early and often. Even if one starts out with a very small amount coming out of each paycheck, the length of time the money is invested and the compounding of interest make it much easier to provide for a comfortable living in the years following retirement. Of course, it takes discipline and commitment to make it happen. But if one begins with the first paycheck to have a certain amount withheld and set aside for those latter years, it will soon not even be missed, and it will grow faster than you might realize. As one gets a raise in pay, part of that raise can be set aside to increase the savings.

Fortunately for reasons I will not go into here, we will live comfortably in retirement; but if I had it to do over, I would certainly start early and save often. Along the way, I had a good friend who was taught by his father to save ten percent of his income, to tithe ten percent of his income, and to live on the other eighty percent. If one starts with that premise, it is amazing how manageable that practice is. We would all find our lives more balanced and more meaningful if we utilized that model. So if I had my ministry to do over, I would handle my income differently. Joye and I covenanted early in our marriage to tithe ten percent of our income, and God has blessed us for that. But I would add to that formula to save ten percent from the beginning.

Chapter XV

TRUSTING GOD

Surely God is my salvation; / I will trust, and will not be afraid, / for the Lord God is my strength and my might; / he has become my salvation. (Isa. 12:2)

If I had my ministry to do over, I would still try to stay in close touch with God to seek and do God's will. But I would try to worry less and trust God more.

One of the most obvious things as I look back across my ministry is the powerful way in which God has blessed the churches that I have had the privilege of serving. Perhaps equally as obvious is the wonderful way in which God has blessed my life. It has been a rich and fulfilling half-century as I have been allowed to be involved in people's lives at crucial moments. No other profession is allowed access to people at so many momentous intersections of their lives.

To be able to rejoice with new parents who have just experienced a miracle from God in the birth of their child is matched only by being able to baptize that baby and help the parents and the congregation to realize their wonderful opportunity and solemn duty to bring up the child in the ways of God. When a couple comes to the pastor to celebrate their marriage in the church, it is a blessed event when the pastor can help them to understand that their lives will be a much stronger bond if God is part of that union. What a joy it is to stand with them before the altar of the church and lead them in taking a vow to "honor and cherish each other" as they place God at the center of their relationship.

Whether it is a child come of age or adults who recognize the need to make a central place for God in their lives, the pastor helps them to understand and formalize their new relationship with God and the church. Early in my ministry I was able to baptize a seventy-eight-year-old man, and I have rejoiced across the years that I was able to help him to come to that decision before his life on earth was over. Then at the most tender moment of all, when a member of the family dies, the pastor gets a call to come to the home or the hospital, to help the family move through this deep loss, and to lead the public and formal celebration of the person's life while pointing to the grace of God in the midst of suffering and death. God has blessed me with these and many other experiences.

But God has also helped churches that I have served overcome discord, grow in number and spirit, organize for ministry in the community and mission in the world, and build edifices to serve their members and the community in which they were placed. God has richly blessed me by calling me to be a part of these communities of faith and to meet the wonderful people who made up the membership of the churches I was privileged to serve.

TRUSTING GOD

At times there were challenges. On occasion I was not sure that we would achieve some goal or overcome some hardship. I must admit that I worked tirelessly to help God get things done. But I should have known that God was able all the time. God was leading the church, and I was sometimes seeking God's will, sometimes working overtime when I should have been praying and trusting God more.

When I look back, I can see that I should have trusted God more. God had everything in control all the time. God may need our help sometimes, but God can and will do far more than we are often willing to give God credit for doing. If I had my ministry to do over, I would still try to stay in close touch with God to seek and do God's will. But I would try to worry less and trust God more. After all, the church is God's and will be until the end of time.

Notes

5. Involving the Laity

1. *The Book of Discipline of The United Methodist Church* (Nashville: The United Methodist Publishing House, 2004), ¶ 125.

10. Personal Devotions

1. Rudy Rasmus, *Touch: The Power of Touch in Transforming Lives* (Baxter Press and Spirit Rising Music, 2006), p. 121.
2. Norman Shawchuck and Reuben P. Job, *A Guide to Prayer for All Who Seek God* (Nashville: Upper Room Books, 2003).